SIX PRINCIPAL RAGAS

SIX PRINCIPAL RAGAS,

WITH A

BRIEF VIEW

OF

HINDU MUSIC.

BY

SOURINDRO MOHUN TAGORE

GYAN

Published by

GYAN

Gyan Publishing House
5, Ansari Road
Daryaganj, New Delhi-110002
Phone: 011-47034999, 9811692060
E-mail: books@gyanbooks.com

Distribution Network
gyanbooks.com
India, USA, Canada, UK, Australia, France

ISBN: 978-81-212-8336-6 (PB)
First Published, 1877

2nd Impression 2023

Printed at: Gyan Press, Delhi.

SIX PRINCIPAL RAGAS
Author: SOURINDRO MOHUN TAGORE

SARASVATI

Lith. and print by K.H. Doss.

Six Principal Ragas,

WITH A

BRIEF VIEW

OF

HINDU MUSIC.

BY

SOURINDRO MOHUN TAGORE, Mus. Doc.,

FOUNDER AND PRESIDENT OF THE BENGAL MUSIC SCHOOL;

Officier d' Académié, Paris; Member of the Royal Asiatic Society, and Fellow of the Royal Society of Literature, Great Britain and Ireland; Associate Member of the Royal Academy of Science, Letters and Fine Arts of Belgium; Member of the Royal Academy of Music, Stockholm, Sweden; Honorary Fellow of the Royal Academy of St. Cecilia, Rome; Socio Onorario Societa Didascalica Italiana; Corresponding Member of the Royal Musical Institute of Florence; Corresponding Member of the Royal Academy of Raffaello, Urbino, Italy; Fellow of the University of Sassari, Sardinia, &c., &c., &c.

[SECOND EDITION.]

Calcutta:

CALCUTTA CENTRAL PRESS COMPANY, LIMITED,

5, COUNCIL HOUSE STREET.

1877.

PREFACE.

WITH a view to imparting His Royal Highness an idea of the Indian Melodies, the Author has set to notation the six principal *Rágas* of the Hindus, adopting their national notation as the one indispensable for the thorough expression of Hindu Music. To impart picturesqueness to the treatise, as well as to clothe it with orientalism, he has also given their emblematical representations. As a preliminary matter, the Introduction treats of topics, a knowledge of which is necessary for the due comprehension of the *Rágas*.

In the Appendix, the Author has noted down a few songs of *Jayadeva*—a true 'poetic child'—to marry at the auspicious moment of the Prince's advent, Music to 'immortal Verse.'

Conscious as the Author is that the offering he brings to the throne, is not worthy of His Royal Highness, he hopes and believes that what may be wanting in the book, will be considered made up for by his devoted loyalty.

INTRODUCTION.

In the acceptation in which it is taken by us, the word *saṅgíta* has a complex signification. It means the union of three things—*gíta*, *vádya* and *nritya*; or *song*, *percussion* and *dancing*. The works that treat of the principles and laws of both vocal and instrumental music, and of the rules and directions with regard to the whole scope of theatric representation, are called *Saṅgíta Śástras*. *Saṅgíta Śástra* may be considered in a two-fold view—as a science and as an art. Considered as a science, it treats of the origin and propagation of *Náda* or sound of the doctrine of *śrutis*, or the theory of *Sañskrita* intervals, of the doctrine of *svaras* or musical sounds, of the formation of the different species of scales, of the rules of *múrchchanás* and *tánas*, of the composition of *rágas* and their various modifications and variations, of the variety of *tálas* or times conformable to regular metre, and of the rules and directions with respect to the various styles of theatric representation. Considered as an art, it lays down the necessary directions for the cultivation of the human voice, for the performance of instrumental music, and for the various motions and gestures in dancing. *Saṅgíta Śástra* is accordingly divided into two portions; namely, *aupapattika* and *kríḍásidaha*, or theoretical and practical. The general and most essential characteristic of *gíta vádya* and *nritya* is *rakti* or the power of affecting the heart.

Of *Sangíta*, there are two descriptions—*Márga* and *Desí*; the former being the style of music invented by the *Rishis* and the *Gandharvas*, and extant among the *Áryyas;* the latter comprising all the various styles of music that obtain in various places. The highest order of music, the *Márga Sangíta*, being of sacred origin, is everywhere the same, and is universally venerated; but the *Desí* styles are of local growth, and are determined by the manners, habits and characters of the people among whom they prevail, each style having its peculiarities. Although the theory of the *Márga Sangíta* has been still preserved in the Sanskrita works on music, yet owing partly to want of cultivation, partly to political influence, and partly to other adventitious circumstances, the practice of it has almost become extinct. *Rágas* and *ráginís*, in these days, are performed without strict regard to the rules laid down by the Sanskrita authorities; while dancing is no more the representation of sacred love and affection which animated the heart of the ancient Hindus.

With regard to the origin of *Sangíta*, we are quite in the dark. In the absence of historic light, all our attempts to penetrate the thick gloom of antiquity prove abortive. The accounts of ancient India are either buried in the abyss of time, or so enveloped in mythical legends that they appear to us too obscure to reason upon. The accounts of the *Puránas* or later religious books of the Hindus, are so wrapped up in mysteries and fables that we can hardly confide in their veracity. It was a very common custom with the ancients to ascribe to divine revelation the invention of all the arts and the sciences of which they possessed no records.

The information which we derive from the *Purána*s on the subject of music have no doubt some pretension at least to authenticity; and gleams of truth may be gained from them. Music in that venerable antiquity was cultivated by the *Rishis* and the *Gandharvas*, who brought it to a considerable degree of improvement. Among inspired mortals, the first musicians are said to have been *Nárada*, *Tumburu*, *Huhu*, and *Bharata*, of whom the last is believed to have reduced it to a proper system, and brought it down to earth from the land of the gods. It may be observed in passing that the allusion to gods probably refers to the *Áryyas* who breathed and thought long before the age of Homer, on the plateau of Central Asia, which is well known to be situated somewhere beyond the Hindukush. The light of revelations and the evidences of ethnology concur in pointing to this spot as the primæval abode of humanity. Philological researches and comparative anatomy tend to confirm the basis on which such a doctrine is made to stand. Placed under a mild climate, and under a strange coincidence of congenial circumstances, the human mind bloomed here in its full vigour and natural freshness. Here sprang that light which illuminates the real history of modern civilization. Here it was that societies were first established, and philosophy, agriculture, and noble arts first received any considerable development. It was in this region that music was cultivated by the holy sages, who are represented by the ancient authorities as gods, in contradistinction to the surrounding people, who were involved in ignorance and barbarism. The *Gandharva Veda*, which is entirely devoted to music, is derived from the *Sáma Veda*, a relic of the Aryan mind—a fact which conclusively proves that Hindu music received a systematic precision even in so high an antiquity as the Vedic age.

Sañgíta Vidyá or music is otherwise called *Náda Vidyá* on account of the whole system of music being evolved from *náda* or sound. *Náda* gives birth to *śrutis* or *enharmonic* genus, which again are the essential elements in the formation of *svaras* or tones; these *svaras*, ranged and disposed in various successions, constitute the variety of *rágas;* and from *rágas, gíta* or songs receive their proper character. It is by *náda* that *vádya* is developed; *gíta* and *vádya* again are the necessary accompaniments of *nritya*. *Nada* therefore underlies the three constituents of *Sañgíta*.

Sañskrit authorities are of opinion that *náda* has its origin in *ákáśa*, the ethereal element which pervades the whole universe; and ascribe this phenomenon to the combined action of fire and air. It may here be observed that the phenomena that were formerly ascribed to fire, are in the present age considered as the effects of heat. Science being then but in its infancy, no wonder that cause and effect would be confounded. It is an experimental fact that fluids in general manifest an expansive motion, on being heated. When any portion of fluid in the atmosphere rapidly expands owing to the increase of temperature, it creates in the surrounding body of air a vibratory motion which is the immediate CAUSE of the phenomenon. We cannot however form an idea of its efficient cause. It appears evident that there is in the *ákáśa* an aptitude to produce *náda,* as well as a capacity in the ear it receive it; but as regards the nature of that aptitude, it is beyond human comprehension in the present system of our existence. This aptitude it is which is probably called by the Sañskrita writers *anáhata* or *ákásasambhava náda.* It is developed into *áhata náda,* by the collision of two objects. It is a matter of every-day experience that whenever two bodies mutually strike each other, an impression is produced on the ear by the vibrations of the air acting upon that organ, and thus we get the idea of *náda.*

According to the manner of its production, *náda* is classified into *káyábhava,* or those that are produced by the human organs of sound, into *vínásambhava,* or the sounds which arise from the vibrations of the strings of musical instruments, and into *vañśadisambhava,* or the sounds proceeding from breathing through the wind instruments.

We shall now exhibit the view of the *Sañskrita* writers on the origin and nature of the vocal sound. In their opinion, vital air or air in the lungs expands rapidly by the action of heat, and in its passage upwards through the mouth, receives a tremulous motion, which is the immediate cause of the *káyábhava náda.* This is a physical question which requires to be elucidated. When air in the lungs grows hot by being suddenly compressed, it gets an expansive motion, and forces its way through an apparatus placed above the windpipe, called larynx or glottis, which regulates the tension of certain vocal chords, and puts them into vibration sufficiently rapid to produce all the various tones of voice.

The human voice is distinguished according to its *grámasthana*, or the appropriate organs which appear most chiefly concerned in its modulation and tone, into *mandra*, *madhya* and *tára*. The *mandra* voice is supposed to proceed almost entirely from the umbilical region, and is designated by the English as the chest voice; the *madhya* voice appears to proceed immediately from the organism of the throat, and is called the throat voice; and the *tára* voice is said to have its origin in some of the cavities of the brain, and is produced by breathing through the nostrils which modulate it by their influence. The tones that are produced in each of these successive places, are severally twice as intense as the similar ones in the former. That these different modifications of sound result from the different adjustments of the vocal mechanism cannot be disputed, but it is difficult to ascertain the precise nature of these particular adjustments. It is necessary here to observe that, when we intend to utter a musical sound, we press together the vocal chords, and stretch them to a definite tension. It is this muscular action which extends the compass of voice, and gives it various degrees of intensity.

Náda begets *śruti*, *śruti* produces *swara*, from *swara* comes *gráma*, from *gráma múrchchhaná*, and *múrchchhaná* gives rise to *tána*. In the three foregoing *grámasthanas*, there are three species of *tána;* in each *tána*, there are *śrutis*, *swaras*, *grámas* and *múrchchhanás* by which *grámas*, are varied. Thus *gíta*, we find, pre-supposes *śrutis*, *swaras*, *grámas* *múrchchhanás* and *tánas*. We shall dwell on these topics as we proceed.

We find some of the European students of Hindu music slow in comprehending the doctrine of *śrutis*. Although they recognise such minute intervals in theory, they insist on the impracticability of managing them to musical advantage. The reason for such misconception is that they are unaccustomed to such nicety of musical progression. A little acquaintance with the practice of our music will convince them not only of the practicability of the feat, but also of the facility with which it may be achieved. The practised musicians among us can bring it about in both vocal and instrumental performance. *Śrutis*, when cleverly managed, never fail to have a most agreeable effect on the ear; though to appreciate them requires a delicacy not usually met with.

Śrutis form the ground-work on which the superstructure of Hindu music is built. All attempts to comprehend its principles without an accurate conception of them, would prove abortive. We therefore intend to give a clear exposition of the nature of *śrutis* and their application in Hindu music.

Śrutis, in the musical acceptation of the term, are particles of sound, perceivable by the ear. They are the essential elements in the formation of the tones of which *saptaka* or octave is composed. They vary in quality or intensity according to the places of their origin; *viz.*, the chest, the throat, and the head; those of the throat vibrating twice as rapidly, and, being consequently twice as intense, as these similar ones of the chest;

and what holds true of this, holds also true of the rest. In each of these places, there are twenty-two kinds of them. It may be observed here that the compass of the Hindu scale is limited to three *saptakas.* The *srutis* of the lowest *saptaka,* which appear to proceed almost entirely from the lungs, are said to belong to the *mandra gráma;* those of the middle *saptaka,* whose appropriate organ appears to be the throat, to the *madhya gráma;* and the *śrutis* of the highest *saptaka* are supposed to be derived from the brain, and are said to dwell in the *tára gráma.* To every one of these places, there are twenty-two strings said to be attached, from which, when struck by the wind, the *śrutis* are said to proceed. These *śrutis* vary the quality of the tones, and rise higher and higher up in succession, and gradually increase in intensity as they extend over different *saptakas.* In *achalthâta,* a species of stringed instrument whose frets are adjusted to the *enharmonic scale,* we perceive them to follow the same law of succession, but they are arranged and disposed in the reverse order. Thus we find that, unlike the *chromatic scale* of the English, which is divided into twelve semi-tones, our octave proceeds by still minuter intervals, called *srutis,* corresponding to the *enharmonic genus* of the Greeks. We shall now exhibit the disposition of *śrutis* in the octave.

We divide the notes of a *saptaka* into twenty-two *śrutis,* by assigning four to *shaja, madhyamar* and *panchama,* which, with the English, are reckoned major tones, three to *rishava* and *dhaivata,* which the English call minor tones, and two to *gandhára* and *nishada,* called by them semi-tones.

We deem it necessary to remark that the term quartertone is used in all English works in the sense of *śruti;* but it is not precisely a quartertone as is generally supposed. It is sometimes a quartertone, and at others the third of a tone, according to its position in the scale. The intervals between *sharja* and *rishava, madhyama* and *panchama, panchama* and *dhaivata,* as we have already stated, are each divided into four *śrutis;* and each *śruti* in these definite places is a quartertone. Likewise there are three *śrutis* between *rishava* and *gándhára* and *dhaivata* and *nishada,* and in these intervals, each *śruti* is the third of a tone. But it should be borne in mind that *śruti* cannot be reckoned quartertone or the third of a tone indiscriminately.

Each of the *śrutis* has a distinct name assigned to it, as is specified in the following table:—

NOTES.		NAMES OF THE COMPRISING ŚRUTIS.
Sharja	...	*Tívrá, Kumudvatí, Mandá, Chhandovatí.*
Rishava	...	*Dayávatí, Ranjaní, Ratiká.*
Gándhára	...	*Raudri, Krodhí.*
Madhyama	...	*Bajriká, Prasariní, Príti, Márjjanú.*
Panchama	...	*Kshiti, Rakta, Sandípaní, Álapaní.*
Dhaivata	...	*Mandantí, Rohiní, Ramya.*
Nishada	...	*Ugrá, Kshobhini.*

We apprehend that the progression by *śrutis* is sufficient to show the relations which the intervals of the notes bear to each other; and that such progression is subservient to all musical purposes. It is capable of producing the simplest as well as the most complex order of music. From the calculation of *śrutis*, as measuring the intervals, different kinds of scales are formed.

Against the foregoing doctrine of *śrutis*, objections are generally urged that it is mathematically inaccurate. But it should be considered that in the arrangement of the intervals, the *Sañskrita* writers were not strictly guided by mathematical calculations, but that they proceeded on principles dictated by their sense of music.

For our own part, we cannot persuade ourselves to believe that mathematics is indispensably necessary for the comprehension of music, though we do not deny the susceptibility of its being subjected to a mathematical test. The principal thing we require in the acquisition of music, is a fine, well-cultivated ear, which enables us to detect and feel the sense of the various tonal combinations. Reducible as its principles are to scientific theories, the comprehension of those principles does not necessarily presuppose a knowledge of mathematics. Sense, we think, is the best judge in this matter.

From the writings of the Oriental scholars of Europe, little information can be derived on the *Sañskrita* doctrine of musical sounds, beyond a cursory notice of it. It shall be at present our endeavour to give in some detail the views of the *Sañskrita* writers, together with our own reflections on the subject.

A *swara* or musical sound is the aggregate result of a number of *śrutis*. It has a calm and soothing influence on the ear, and in this particular it is that it differs from all other sounds. The *swaras* or notes are in number the same as in the music of the West, and are named and disposed in the following order:—

Sharja, rishava, gándhára, madyama, panchama, dhaivata, and *nishada*, of which the initial letters are taken in *swarasadhana* or solmization, and serve to exhibit the *swaragráma* or gamut, otherwise called *saptaka*. It stands as follows: *sa, ri, ga, ma, pa, dha, ni*, very nearly resembling the major mode of the English, *ut, ri, mi, fa, sol, la, si, ut*.

We learn from the *Sañskrita* writers that the various gradations of sounds constituting the *swaragráma* were originally derived from the cries of animals and the song of birds. The *sharja*, they say, was imitated from the call of the peacock; the *rishava*, from the bellowing of the ox; the *gándhára*, from the bleating of the goat; the *madhyama*, from the howling of the jackal, or from the voice of the crane; the *panchama*, from the call of the black bird, called *kokhila;* the *dhaivata*, from the sound of the frog, or from the neighing of the horse; and the *nishada*, from the noise of the elephant.

Men generally question the truth of this statement which, in their estimation, is a mere fable, originating in the minds of the *Sañskrita* writers. However paradoxical this may at first appear, we intend to make some observations on this point, which may, to a great extent, unravel the mystery.

There is nothing in nature that calls forth our attention, or rouses our feeling so quickly as sound. In the primitive stage of society, when man led a rural life, nothing interested him so much as the cries of animals and the song of birds. Placed from their infancy within the reach of these sounds, they soon learnt to discern certain minute musical intervals, which are the germs of melody, and from which, in process of time, the *suddha swaragráma* or natural scale was evolved. We shall now cite a passage from an eminent authority to bear on our position. "The sounds of animated nature, especially the songs of birds, appear to be another source from which the formation of peculiar scales has been originally derived. The melodious notes of singing birds delight the savage as well as, and perhaps even more than the civilized man who cultivates music as an art. The former is familiar with them from his childhood. He unconsciously receives his musical instruction in the field and forest. The natural instinct for imitation, generally so powerful in the savage, soon leads him to produce intervals similar to those which he hears. He finds his success in the chase facilitated by imitating the sounds of the animals which he desires to capture. His imitation must be so exact as to be deceptive. Thus his ear and his voice are practised and become accustomed to certain minute intervals, which are involuntarily transferred by him to his primitive songs, and from which, in the course of time, a fixed order of intervals is developed, and gradually extended to the octave, constituting a scale." Among various transcripts of the voice of nature, which have been recorded in notation, we shall transcribe here only one or two instances, to show that music owes its origin to the simple and immutable expressions of animated nature, and that we derive many hints for musical composition from them.

Ox.

It should be admitted that the intervals of the *saptaka* have not been hit upon by lucky chance; but that they have been discerned by extensive observation. From the calls of animated nature, the musical observers of antiquity ascertained the different gradations of sound that are practically employed in music, and found them all to fall under seven divisions, which are called the seven degrees of notes. Such is the law of nature that the gradation next above the seventh degree is similar to, though it is higher than, the first of the series of seven degrees. This principle of nature could not long have escaped the attention of the ancient Hindus, as these degrees of notes are said to occur in the *Sáma Veda* in their persent order. It is indeed astonishing how they could, in such a remote antiquity, acquire a truth which has been arrived at by the Europeans only at a recent period after long scientific investigation; and what is more so is, that our *saptaka* has received such a scientific precision that, if *dha* is rendered but one *śruti* lower in the scale, it coincides with the *diatonic scale* of the Europeans. From the above circumstances, it must be inferred that the intervals of the *saptaka* have not been arbitrarily chosen; but that they must have been selected on certain principles derived from the science of acoustics. But in the arrangement of them, the *Sañskrita* writers have been guided not by mathematical calculations, but by that higher faculty, called artistic consciousness. For the purpose of avoiding the tedious principles of ratios and proportions, they have adopted the easy convention of dividing the *saptaka* into *śrutis*. It should be observed here that the principles which form the science of acoustics enter into Hindu music, though they are different in form from those of the European system. The science of acoustics, as it exists among us, is subservient to all the purposes of music.

A *saptaka* is the aggregate of the seven intervals from the first of a series to its repetition in the next. The *Sañskrita* writers have taken cognizance of enly three *saptakas*, the human organism of voice being too feeble to produce more. These are designated *mandra*, *madhya*, and *tára*, according to the places of their origin. The *Vedantists* have also made mention of only three *saptakas*, which are respectively called by them *anudátya*, *sarit*, and *udátya*. But the compass of a singer's voice upon the musical scales, in general, does not exceed two and half *saptakas*, some being able to sing distinctly the interval between the first note of the *mandra saptaka*, and the fourth note of the *tára saptaka*; others, that between the fourth note of the *mandra saptaka*, and the last note of the *tára saptaka*. Instrumental music being but an imitation of the vocal one, our *vina* and other instruments are generally adjusted to two and half *saptakas.* In fact, this extent of notes is quite sufficient for all the purposes of Hindu music.

We shall now give the reader a general idea of the *kákalí swaras* or supplementary notes, called flats and sharps, with all the clearness that the subject admits of. When they undergo changes in their natural compass, the notes of the *saptaka* are divided into twelve *kákali* or *vikrita swaras,* forming our *vikrita swaragráma,* analogous to the *chromatic scale* of the English. These *vikritas* are met with, when the adoption of any other key than *sharja* varies the modulation, and brings about changes in the disposition of *śrutis.* Of these, there are two descriptions; namely, *komalas* and *tívras ; i. e.,* flats and sharps. We may want to render a note somewhat higher, or somewhat deeper. When it is raised to one or more *śrutis* of the succeeding interval, it is said to be rendered *tívra* or sharp; on the other hand, it is said to be rendered *komala* or flat, when it is depressed by one or more *śrutis* of the preceding interval.

It is necessary to observe here that any sound possessing musical quality is styled *swara.* It does not receive the character of *suddha swara,* or natural tone, unless it possess its full complement of *śrutis.* *Suddha swaras* differ from *swaras,* chiefly by being prolonged so as to give the ear a more decided perception of their height, formation and relation to each other. *Sharja,* for instance, is the mere name of a *swara.* When it is heightened so as to contain four complete *śrutis,* then and not till then can it be designated *suddha* or natural *sharja*. Let us now illustrate the process by which the seven notes of the original scale are formed into twelve *vikritas*. In the first *tetrachord*, if *ri* is rendered two *śrutis* lower in the scale, and reckoned as the key note; *i.e.*, when *sharja* loses two from its full complement of *śrutis* to *rishava*, the first note becomes possessed of two, and is rendered *vikrita* by being reduced to a semi-tone; and possessed of four *śrutis*, *ri* at the same time becomes *vikrita*, by being increased to a major tone. *Ri* gains two *śrutis* from *sa*, yet it loses one to *ga*, and retains only four. Gaining one *śruti* from *ri*, *ga* becomes possessed of three; *i.e.*, the interval between *ga* and *ma* becomes a minor tone. *Ma* partakes of the nature of *sa* in both its *suddha* and *vikrita* or natural and artificial condition. It is generally rendered *vikrita* by being possessed of two *śrutis*; *i.e.*, by being reduced to a semi-tone.

Now let us consider what happens in the second *tetrachord*. In the *madhyama gráma*, *pa* becomes possessed of three *śrutis*, and is reduced to a minor tone; and *dha*, gaining one from *pa*, becomes possessed of four *śrutis*, and is rendered *vikrita* by being increased to a major tone. Taking two *śrutis* from the *vikrita dhaivata*, *ni* at the same time becomes *kákali*; *i.e.*, the interval between *dha* and *ni* is reduced to a semi-tone, and that between *ni* and *sa* increased to a major tone.

The scale therefore would stand thus:—

Sa ... *Ri* .. *Ga* . *Ma* ... *Pa* ... *Dha* .. *Ni* . *Sa*

Ri♭ *Ga*♭ *Ma*♯ *Dha*♭ *Ni*♭

Hence we find that our *vikrita swaragráma* differs from the English *chromatic scale* in this, that the former proceeds by semi-tones aud *śrutis*, while the latter, by a regular succession of semi-tones. It should be remarked that when we adopt any other note than *sharja* as the key-note, we find it necessary to interpose *komalas* and *tíbras ; i.e.*, flats and sharps, according as the modulation may require one or the other, between various notes of the *sharjagráma* or natural scale; and ultimately we find that it is divided into twelve *vikritas* or artificial notes. These together with seven natural notes number nineteen.

Their fondness for fiction and mythology led the *Sañskrita* writers to adopt allegories in their classification of notes. In consideration of their nature and extent, the notes were ranged under four castes; namely, *Bráhmana, Kshatriya, Vaisya* and *Sudra.* Possessed of four *śrutis*, and therefore considered as principal notes, *sharja, madhyama, and panchama* are placed in the first class. Next in order come *rishava* and *dhaivata,* composed as they are of three *śrutis.* To the third class are assigned *gándhára* and *nishάda,* by reason of their containing only two *śrutis.* In the last class are placed the *kákalí swaras,* they being very minute divisions of notes. In assigning the notes to different castes, the *Sañskrita* writers were prompted by no other motive than to distinguish their different classes; the principle being analogous to, if not the same with, that on which in Western music they are arranged under four heads; namely, the major tones, the minor tones, the semi-tones, and the artificial or *chromatic* notes.

With reference to their application in the composition of *rágas*, these notes are considered under four aspects: *bádí*, *sambádí*, *anubádí* and *bibádí*. On this subject, the information that has been furnished by the orientalists, is quite inadequate to enlighten the readers. It is our intention, and it shall be our endeavour, to give them a clear notion of these different kinds of notes, and to set forth the rules for ascertaining them as laid down by the *Sañskrita* authorities.

The laws with regard to *bádí*, *sambádí*, *anubádí* and *bibadí* guide us in the discernment and choice of those notes which are essentially important in the formation of *rágas*, and which immediately determine their true nature; of those which should be admitted, and of those which should be rejected in order to avoid offending the ear by incoherence. These laws, in short, are strictly observed in the melodic progression of a *rága* which loses its agreeable effect when any of them is least infringed. We find a parallel practice obtaining among the ancient Greeks under the name of *petteia*, a part of *melopœia*, which taught them what sounds they should reject, what they should admit, and what they ought to employ most frequently.

By *bádí* is meant that note which is always of the greatest utility in the formation of a *rága*, and immediately ascertains its peculiar character. Owing to its most frequent use and permanency, it predominates over all the other notes that are admitted into a *rága*, and plays the most important part. It behoves us to remark here that in *rágabistára*, or the extension of a *rága*, the performer may use any of the subordinate notes he chooses more copiously than the leading or essential note; but it is not entitled to the name of *bádiswara*, by reason of its failing in the other requirement—permanency. Such notes are considered mere accidental or transient ones, they only gliding upon the melodic progression without ever forming essential parts of it. From the interpretation given to the term in the *Sangíta Darpana*, it appears that *bádi* is derived from the word *badana*, which means the power of producing *rágas*; and the note possessing it, is donominated the *bádiswara*. The next important note is called *sambádi*. It is homogeneal to *bádi*, and has a strong affinity with it. *Sambádi* is a great auxiliary to *bádi* in announcing the nature of a *rága*. Less in importance as it is than the leading note, it is less copiously employed than the latter, but more copiously than other subordinate notes. The latter are called *anubádi*, inasmuch as they immediately precede or follow the essential notes to which they are attached, and severally contribute, to some extent, to the development of a *rága*. They are in their nature the means between the two extremes—concord and discord. The last description of notes; *i.e.*, *bibádi*, analogous to the *antiphonia* of the Greeks, is such a note as appears to the ear dissonant, and if employed in any *rága*, with which it is incompatible, destroys its melodious effect. The *bádi* is aptly represented as the sovereign; the *sambádi*, as the *mantri* or prime minister; the *anubádi*, as his attendants; and the *bibádi*, as his enemy.

It is by the aforesaid laws that we are also enabled to ascertain the relation of agreement or of disagreement between any two notes.

The notes possessing the same aggregate of *śrutis* are denominated *sambádí*; as for example, *śa* and *pa*, *ṛi* and *dha*, *ga* and *ni*, *ma* and *śa*. This rule is not without exception. Although both *ma* and *pa* consists of four *śrutis*, yet as they are consecutive to each other, they do not pass for *sambádí*. The foregoing rule also serves to ascertain the notes related as *sambádí*, when the change of scale requires a different modulation. For instance, should we adopt *pa* as the keynote, *ṛi* of the original scale would become *pa* in the new scale. Thus we see *ṛi* and *pa*, possessed of the same complement of *śrutis*, become *sambádí* or consonant. The *Saṅgíta Darpaṇa* has laid down another rule for ascertaining *sambádí* notes—a rule which has a direct application in both the natural scale and that formed by the change of key. The notes having eight or twelve *śrutis* intervening between them are related as *sambádí*; as for example, *ṛi* and *pa*, *ni* and *ma* sharp, &c. Both the rules, we think, have the same bearing, and may be included under the following general rule:—

Such notes are considered as *sambádí* as are so related to each other, that if the former is adopted as the keynote, the latter becomes the fourth in the ascending scale; whereas, if the latter is taken as the fundamental note, the former becomes the fifth in the descending scale, as appears from the following diagram:—

```
Sa . . . Ri . . Ga . Ma . . . Pa
         |      |        |    |
         Sa     Ri       Ga   Ma
         |      |        |    |
         Pa     Dha      Ni   Sa
```

In the opinion of the *Sañskrita* writers, every two successive notes are always *bibádi* or dissonant; for instance, *dha* and *ni*, *ri* and *ga*, and so forth. The author of the *Sangíta Darpana* holds that the notes having one *srutis* intervening between them, are also *bibádi*. In the opinion of the *Sangíta Ratnabali*, the notes having thirteen *srutis* intervening between them, are considered as *anubádi;* and those having nine *srutis* intervening between them, as *bibádi*.

Harmony, in its modern import, is not admissible, nor is it of much importance in Hindu music; its predominant character being melody. Although notes may be combined as in harmony, conformably to the laws of *bádi*, *sambádi*, *anubádi* and *bibádi*, yet such *chords* when set to *rágas* and *ráginís*, far from improving and flourishing them, would rather infringe their genuine character. Mr. Willard and other eminent European authorities also subscribe to this position. With regard to the admissibility of harmony into our music, Captain Willard truly observes: "Indeed, so wide is the difference between the natures of the European and Oriental music, that I conceive a great many of the latter would baffle the attempts of the most expert contrapunist to set a harmony to them, by the existing rules of that science." Nevertheless, Hindu music is not altogether void of harmony. Although harmony is not employed in our vocal performance, yet it is used, though very sparingly, in *sristálañkára*, a kind of instrumental grace. To explain the nature of the chords, as they are employed in Hindu music, let us distinguish between the concords of harmony and those of melody. The former are the agreeable consonances of simultaneous notes; but these are not strictly applicable to melody, which is the agreeable relation of successive notes, and whose excellence and beauty depend on the regular disposition of chords through which it is made to pass. Such is the mechanism of the ear, that the impression of the notes which have been just heard, linger in the ear for a time sufficiently long to be blended with those that succeed, and thus to produce the effects of true harmony. T. Perronet Thompson, an ingenious writer, truly observes: "The reason why the intervals that produce harmony, produce also melody, seems to be, that *melody is retrospective harmony*, or depends on a perception of harmonical relation to sounds that have preceded. * * * * * * * * * * * The memory of the sounds which have just passed us, linger in the ear, and are accommodated with harmonious combinations in those that follow."

Gráma, in the musical acceptation of the term, signifies a series of notes arranged and disposed according to certain laws. It furnishes the basis in which the *śrutis*, notes and *múrchchhanás* inhere. In fact, the *gráma* is the condition of *múrchchhanás*; but for it, their very reality would have been impossible. As the sounds in the *gráma* ascend and descend in succession towards acuteness and gravity, the *múrchchhanás* naturally begin to exist. There are three such in Hindu music; and, in the opinion of some of the *Sañskṛita* authorities, these are *sharjagráma*, *madhyamagráma* and *gándháragráma*, of which the last has now fallen into disuse.

We shall now attempt to exhibit the different modulations of the three *grámas*; *i.e.*, the different dispositions of *śrutis* in the scales; and explain the rules laid down by *Sañskṛita* writers with regard to the deduction of the *madhyama* and *gándháragrámas* from the *sharjagráma*.

Sharjagráma is defined by the author of *Sangíta Darpana* and other *Sañskrita* authorities as the scale wherein *panchama* remains *nirvikarí* or natural; *i.e.*, keeps its proper position in the scale, and retains its full complement of *srutis*; and *madhyamagráma*, as that wherein the fifth note loses one to *dha* from its full complement of *srutis*, and is reduced to a minor tone. Let us now consider the foregoing definition in its full bearing.

It may be asked—why do the *Sañskrita* writers make the *panchama* and not any other note the basis of their definition? The reason is very clear. The first four notes are natural alike in both the *grámas*; it is in the fifth note that change first occurs in the *madhyamagráma*—a change by which it is distinguished from all other scales.

The foregoing definition of the *madhyamagráma* may at the first sight appear to be inexhaustive, inasmuch as it does not include the change which *ni* undergoes by being rendered two *srutis* lower in the scale. But it should be remembered that the reduction of *pa* to a minor tone, precludes the necessity of mentioning the other change, as it will, under the law of progression by *srutis*, follow as a necessary sequence. The following diagram will show the arrangement of *srutis* in the *sharjagráma* and how *madhyamagráma* is deduced from it:—

Sharjagráma	*Sa* . . .	*Ri* . .	*Ga* .	*Ma* . . .	*Pa* . . .	*Dha* . .	*Ni* .	*Si* . . .	*Ri* . .	*Ga*.
Madhyamagráma	...	...		*Sa*	*Ri*	*Ga*	*Ma*	*Pa*	*Dha*	*Ni*.

From the above diagram, it appears that the *sharjagráma* consists of two disjunct, but perfectly similar *tetrachords* separated by a major tone. From this, the *madhyamagráma* is deduced by the diminution of the interval between *pa* and *dha* by one *śruti*, and by rendering *ni* two *śrutis* lower in the scale. Thus we find that the interval between *pa* and *dha* is reduced to a minor tone, and esteemed as *rishava;* and the interval between *dha* and *ni* to a semi-tone. In this case, the interval between *dha* and *ni* being a semi-tone, that between *ni* and *sa* must be a major tone; and it is considered as *madhyama.*

We shall now attempt to explain the construction of the *gándhára-gráma,* and the peculiar changes set forth by the *Saṅgíta Darpana* in the disposition of the *śrutis* in the scale.

Gándháragráma is deduced from the primary *gráma,* and not from the *madhyamagráma,* as is supposed. If *ga* takes one *śruti* from *ri,* and another from *ma,* and becomes thus possessed of four; or in other words, *ri* being lowered by one *śruti,* and *ma* raised by one *śruti,* if the interval between *ga* and *ma* becomes a major tone, the scale formed with reference to it as the key-note, is denominated the *gándháragráma.* It is necessary to remark here, that *gándhára* to be the *gráma* or fundamental note, should be reckoned as *sharja,* and, as a matter of course, should consist of four *śrutis.* The other changes characteristic of the scale are as follows:—

1*st.*—The four *srutis* of *madhyama* from the interval between the fourth and the fifth in the *sharjagráma;* by giving one to *ga*, it consists of three *srutis; i.e.*, it is reduced to a minor tone.

2*nd.*—*Ni* takes one *sruti* from *dha*, and another from *sa*, and becomes thus possessed of four; or in other words, *ni* being depressed by one *sruti* in the scale, and *sa* raised one *sruti* higher, the interval between *ni* and *sa* is increased to a major tone.

3*rd.*—*Sa* losing to *ni* one from its full complement of *srutis*, retains three; *i.e.*, by rendering *sa* higher by one *sruti*, the interval between *sa* and *ri* is reduced to a minor tone, and taken as *dhaivata.*

There is another change yet to be mentioned. *Dha* taking two *srutis* from *pa*, reduces it to a semi-tone, and losing one to *ni*, becomes itself possessed of four *srutis*. But this change is not peculiar to this *gráma*. The following diagram will show how *gándháragráma* is formed from the *sharjagráma*:—

Sharjagráma *Sa* . . . *Ri* . . *Ga* . *Ma* . . . *Pa* . . . *Dha* . . *Ni* . *Sa* . . . *Ri.*

Gándháragráma *Sa* *Ri* *Ga* *Ma* *Pa* *Dha* *Ni.*

We hold with the author of *Ratnabali* and several other *Sañskrita* authorities that the word *gráma* denotes the note in reference to which the relative heights and distances of the six other notes of the octave are ascertained. The three *grámas* considered in Hindu music, are nothing but the first or lowest notes of the three *saptakas* to which the whole compass of the Hindu scale is limited. The very interpretation of the word *sharja* implies that it is the foundation of the *saptaka*. In so far as they pre-suppose a *sharja*, the other notes do not admit of being taken as *grámas*. Each of the other notes, considered apart from some *sharja* underlying it, may be taken as *sharja* itself. From the above circumstances, we are warranted to conclude that *sharja* is unquestionably the primary *gráma*, in the strict sense of the term, and that all other notes are not entitled to bear the name. Such being the case, we may be asked why are then some of the instruments tuned in fourths and fifths? Properly considered, each of the other notes may be adopted as the key-note. The scales which may be thus formed, are not, strictly speaking, *grámas*, but are esteemed as *thatas* or modes. The reason why the *víná* is tuned in fourths is clear from the nature of the instrument. It has been already stated that, although the three *saptakas* to which the whole scope of Hindu music is confined, are considered as natural, yet the human organism of voice is not so powerful as to produce more than 2½ *saptakas*. In imitation of vocal music, the finger-boards of our instruments also are adjusted so as to exhibit the same extent of notes. Such being the case, *ma*, which occupies the middle position in the octave; *i.e.*, between two perfectly similar *tetrachords*, must be adopted as the key-note; otherwise the compass of notes would either fall short of or exceed 2½ *saptakas*, allowable in practice. To be more explicit; should *víná*, instead of being tuned in fourths, be successively tuned in thirds, seconds,

&c., the extent of notes would fall short of $2\frac{1}{2}$ *saptakas;* and again, should it be tuned in fifths, sixths, &c., the extent would by degrees exceed the limit. It is in consequence of this limitation, that *ma* has been taken as the fundamental note in preference to others. We should therefore persuade ourselves to believe that *madhyamagráma* originated in the peculiar construction of certain favorite musical instruments of the Hindus. Another, and perhaps the chief reason for *ma* being adopted as the *gráma,* appears to be that it is *sambádí* or concordant to *sa,* the primary *gráma;* and that the scale formed with it requires very few *víkrita swaras* or supplementary notes. For the same reason *pa* is also reckoned by some as a secondary *gráma.*

In the whole compass of the Hindu scale, there are twenty-one *múrchchhanás* each *saptaka* containing seven. To exhibit them, a little dexterity is required. When each of the notes of the three *saptakas* is individually produced, it cannot be named *múrchchhaná.* By this term we mean the extending of a note to another in the ascending as well as in the descending scale, without any intermediate break in the disposition of the *srutis* in the interval. In the production of *múrchchhanás,* contiguity between the different degrees of notes is strictly observed; for a least interruption in the continuous flow of the *srutis* that run through them, detracts much from the beauty and agreeableness of the *rágas,* wherein *múrchchhanás* are employed. The *múrchchhaná* is defined by the author of the *Sangíta Darpana* to be the ascension or the descension of the seven notes in succession in the scale, which renders them fit for producing the *rágas.* The *múrchchhanás* are, in fact, the essential ornaments of *rágas,* and contribute in no scanty measure to their extension and development. *Rágas* without *múrchchhanás* are as flowers without fragrance. In *álapa* too, they play an important part.

Múrchchhanás may arise from any of the three *grámasthánas.* But it is the practice with us to commence the *múrchchhaná* of the *sharja-gráma* from the first note of the middle octave, and that of the *madhyamagráma* from the fourth note. The following tables will show the different *múrchchhanás* of the two *grámas,* with the names assigned to them:—

The Múrchchhanás of Sharjagráma.							*Their names.*
Sa.	*Ri.*	*Ga.*	*Ma.*	*Pa.*	*Dha.*	*Ni.*	*Uttarayatá.*
Ni.	*Sa.*	*Ri.*	*Ga.*	*Ma.*	*Pa.*	*Dha.*	*Uttara Mandrá.*
Dha.	*Ni.*	*Sa.*	*Ri.*	*Ga.*	*Ma.*	*Pa.*	*Ranjaní.*
Pa.	*Dha.*	*Ni.*	*Sa.*	*Ri.*	*Ga.*	*Ma.*	*Manjarí.*
Ma.	*Pa.*	*Dha.*	*Ni.*	*Sa.*	*Ri.*	*Ga.*	*Aswakrántá.*
Ga.	*Ma.*	*Pa.*	*Dha.*	*Ni.*	*Sa.*	*Ri.*	*Abhiruhitá.*
Ri.	*Ga.*	*Ma.*	*Pa.*	*Dha.*	*Ni.*	*Sa.*	*Suddhasharjá.*

The Múrchchhanás of Madhyamagráma.							*Their names.*
Ma.	*Pa.*	*Dha.*	*Ni.*	*Sa.*	*Ri.*	*Ga.*	*Saubiri.*
Ga.	*Ma.*	*Pa.*	*Dha.*	*Ni.*	*Sa.*	*Ri.*	*Drabirasvá.*
Ri.	*Ga.*	*Ma.*	*Pa.*	*Dha.*	*Ni.*	*Sa.*	*Kalopantá.*
Sa.	*Ri.*	*Ga.*	*Ma.*	*Pa.*	*Dha.*	*Ni.*	*Natika.*
Ni.	*Sa.*	*Ri.*	*Ga.*	*Ma.*	*Pa.*	*Dha.*	*Suddhamadhyá.*
Dha.	*Ni.*	*Sa.*	*Ri.*	*Ca.*	*Ma.*	*Pa.*	*Íshtá.*
Pa.	*Dha.*	*Ni.*	*Sa.*	*Ri.*	*Ga.*	*Ma.*	*Paurabí.*

We need not exhibit the *múrchchhanás* of the *gandharagráma*, as it has fallen into disuse. As an instance of the *múrchchhanás* of the scale which comprises six notes, those of a scale from which *ni* has been left out, are represented below :—

							Names.
.	*Dha.*	*Pa.*	*Ma.*	*Ga.*	*Ri.*	*Sa.*	*Chaturmasya.*
Dha.	*Pa.*	*Ma.*	*Ga.*	*Ri.*	*Sa.*	0	*Sambhásya.*
Pa.	*Ma.*	*Ga.*	*Ri.*	*Sa.*	0	*Dha.*	*Artha.*
Ma.	*Ga.*	*Ri.*	*Sa.*	0	*Dha.*	*Pa.*	*Chaturtha.*
Ga.	*Ri.*	*Sa.*	0	*Dha.*	*Pa.*	*Ma.*	*Sautramoni.*
Ri.	*Sa.*	0	*Dha.*	*Pa.*	*Ma.*	*Ga.*	*Chitra.*
Sa.	0	*Dha.*	*Pa.*	*Ma.*	*Ga.*	*Ri.*	*Udbhida.*

Múrchchhaná is distinct from *gamaka* with which it is generally confounded, the latter being a tremulous motion of voice, produced by the rapid contraction and extension of the vocal chords. The *gamaka* is nothing but the reiteration of the same note. It is one of the several graces used in Hindu music, and plays an important part in the manifestation of a *rága*. We shall now describe the manner of producing *múrchchhaná* in vocal as well as in instrumental performance. In the former, the vowel sound of the letter from which the *múrchchhaná* commences, is continued to the note to which it is intended to extend, in one unbroken stream of voice; while in the latter, the *múrchchhaná* is produced by the string relating to any fret being drawn out with pressure, either by the forefinger, or by the middle finger, to express any of the succeeding notes to which it should extend.

Múrchchhanás may be brought about not only in the natural scale, but also in the *vikṛita swaragráma* or artificial scale. In all we have fifty-seven pieces of *múrchchhanás* in the whole scope of the Hindu scale, both natural and artificial. In each of them, there are sixty-three pieces of *alaṅkáras*, or excellent, orderly arrangement of notes. Of the various styles of *alaṅkáras*, two instances only are given below:—

Sa ri sa ri ga, ri ga ri ga ma, ga ma ga ma pa, ma pa ma pa dha, pa dha pa dha ni, dha ni dha ni sa.

Sa sa, ri ri, ga ga, ma ma, pa pa, dha dha, ni ni, sa sa.

By *mátrá*, the *Sanskṛita* grammarians mean the measure of time in pronouncing a vowel sound. According to the authors of *Baidyashastras* or medical treatises, it signifies the brief space of time occupied by a single beating of the pulse, or by the twinkling of an eye. But in the import attached to it in some of the musical treatises, the term denotes five times the length of a short vowel. Thus, we find there is a diversity of opinion as to the acceptation of the word *mátrá.* But whatever be the meaning assigned to it by others, in our opinion, the musicians may take any equal interval of time as a *mátrá.* The grammarians reckon four sorts of *mátrás;* namely, *laghu, guru, pluta* and *ardha;* but in *Sangita,* besides these, a fifth named *anu* is included. The *laghu mátrá* is the measure of time in uttering a short vowel; *guru mátrá* is double the length of a *laghu mátrá* or simple sound; the *pluta* is the protracted sound, being three or more times the length of a short vowel; and the *ardha* and the *anu mátrá* are respectively half and one-fourth of a *laghu mátrá.* In the present practice, the performers may adjust the value of a *mátrá* to his will and intention; but whatever be the quantity of duration he would assign to it, the *guru, pluta, ardha* and *anu mátrás* should be taken in proportion to its value. These different descriptions of *mátrás* are indispensably necessary for regulating the course of *śrutis, múrchchhanás, tánas, álápas, gítas* and *chchanda* or rhythm; and constitute an essential of music.

Time in Hindu music is named *tála.* The *tálas* widely differ from the modern measures of European music. They rather resemble, though not in every respect, the rhythmical measures of the Ancients. Our *tála* is metrically divided by a certain arrangement of *mátrás;* whereas 'Time' in the modern music of the Western nations, observes no such division. The word *tála* simply means the beating of time by clapping the hands. To give an accurate idea of its general signification in music, some preliminary observation is necessary. The eternal duration of time is in *Sanskrita* called *laya*. It is beyond the power of the human intellect to conceive of such a thing independently of the external events. When any portion of infinite time is determined by the succession of two events, we are enabled to recognise it. In the acceptation in which it is taken in music, the word *laya* signifies the stream of time that runs through a piece or composition from the instant of its adoption to that when it is dropped. There are three kinds of it reckoned in music; namely, *bilambita, madhya* and *druta*. The *bilambita* and the *madhya laya* are respectively the slower and the quicker course of time, in respect of its normal movement, the *madhya laya*. It is when *laya* is measured conformably to *chhanda*, or regular and symmetrical arrangement of *mátrás* that it can be construed to mean *tála*; and as a matter of course, the movement of *tála* is determined by that of *laya*. *Tála* follows *chhanda*, and is employed to guide its movement. It is a practice with us to beat time with a strict regard to the *mátrás* to which measures are restricted, in order to see whether the *chhanda* of a piece is moving on its proper course. Properly speaking, *tála* is synonymous with *chhanda* or regular metre. It is from *chhanda* that *gíta* derives that regularity and symmetry which pervade it. Music without *chhanda* is just as body without soul, or coloring in painting without design. It is of such importance, that, without it, music loses all its power over the human passions. With regard to the utility of *chhanda* in music, Nathan truly observes: "Music is designated for nobler purposes than merely to please the ear; she is intended to speak to the judgment. But unaided by good poetry, her spell is partly broken, and the bright wreath of her fame droops and withers. Pure composition unites music and poetry in indissoluble bonds; and so intimate is their connection, so equal their value, so indispensable the strictness of their union, that the rules of sense and propriety render them the echo of each other."

It should be here observed that at least four *mátrás* are requisite for constituting a measure; for less than that number passes away too swiftly to enable us to perceive *laya*. We are accustomed to beat time by means of certain conventional words and letters; and the act of doing so is called *sangata*. There are various styles of *sangata*, according to the variety of *chhanda*.

We generally find that the Europeans who have devoted themselves to the researches of Hindu music, widely differ in their opinion as to the import of the terms *rága* and *rágini*; but none has, it seems, attained any thing like an accurate idea of them. It is our intention, and it shall be our attempt, therefore, to elucidate this obscure but important subject, and to give some idea of their peculiar nature. Nathan, a renowned author of European music, holds that *rága* signifies major mode, and *rágini* a minor mode. In the opinion of Sir William Jones, the word *rága* has also the same bearing. J. F. Danneley, in his Encyclopædia of

Music, says: "A mode or scale is called *major*, when its third diatonic note is composed of four chromatic degrees; or is the fifth diatonic-chromatic note of the scale, called also the *major third*; as, C—natural E—natural, C—sharp E—sharp, &c." He further observes: "A mode or scale is said to be minor when the third note, called the minor third, is composed of but three chromatic degrees; as C E—flat, D F—natural; in opposition to major, the third note of which is composed of four chromatic degrees." But the acceptation in which *rága* and *rágiṇí* are taken by us, widely differs from the aforesaid definitions, a mode rather resembling our *ṭháṭa*. We shall here cite a passage from Captain Willard, an accomplished scholar of Hindu music, to bear out our opinion. He says: "The word 'mode' may be taken in two different significations, the one employing manner of style, and the other a key; and, strictly speaking, this latter is the sense in which it is usually understood in music. Mode in the language of the musicians of this country (India) is in my opinion *termed ṭháṭa*, and not *rága* or *rágiṇí*."

In the opinion of Dr. Cary, the word *rága* signifies tune. But Willard says: "It is not strictly a tune according to the acceptation of the word." Danneley defines tune as follows: "The most general idea attached to this word is that of piece of music composed of a certain number of melodic phrases joined by regular and symmetrical forms and terminating in the same key with which it begins." But *rága*, according to its imports in Hindu music, does not strictly observe any such regularity and symmetry in its composition; nor does it always being with the key in which it terminates. How can then the term, "tune," be considered synonymous with *rága?* It is somewhat like our *gata.* A *gata* is rhythmically divided by *tála;* as a tune is divided into equal portions by bars. In a Hindu *rága,* there is no fixed rule with regard to *tála* or rhythmical progression; and, as a matter of course, it needs not to be divided by bars, which mark the exact measurement of time. *Tála* is essentially necessary for the formation of a *gata;* while no such necessity exists with regard to *rágas.* The different kinds of sounds; namely, the short, the long, and the protracted, ranged and disposed in various successions, regular and irregular, suffice to constitute *rágas;* nor can *rága* be construed into song; since various songs may be set to a particular *rága.* On this point, Willard truly observes:— "It is not likewise a song, for able performers can adapt the words of a song to any *ráginí;* nor does a change of time destroy its inherent quality, although it may so far disguise the *ráginí* before an inexperienced ear as to appear a different one." It is when words are set to a *rága,* and when rhythm given to it, that it can mean a song.

Again, *rága* is not *tháta,* as some suppose. *Tháta* is not a *Sañskrita* but a *Prákrita* word, and means a mould. As in a mould, certain ingredients, variously mingled, may be wrought into articles of various kinds, so in a *tháta,* the notes, arranged in different but peculiar orders of succession ascending or descending, with their various *múrchchhanás* may be formed into a variety of *rágas.*

The following extract from Willard will corroborate our position :—
"As amongst us there are two modes, the major and the minor, so the natives have a certain number of *thátas*, to each of which two or more *rágas* or *ráginís* are appropriated. If these signified mode, each should require a different arrangement, which is certainly not the case. Any one may convince himself of this, by procuring a performer on the Sitar. This instrument has movable frets that are shifted from their places, so that when the instrument is properly adjusted, the fingers of the left hand running over them produce those tones only which are proper for the mode to which the frets have been transferred, and no other. Let the Sitar-player be desired to play something in the *rágini Áláhiyá*, and after he has done that, tell him to play some other *rágini* without altering the frets, and it will be seen that other *ráginis* may be performed on the same *tháta*. On the other hand, after he has played *Áláhiyá*, let him play *Lalita* or *Bhairavi* or *Káphi*, *&c.*, *&c.*, and he will be obliged to alter the *tháta* or mode by shifting the frets. A *tháta* comes nearest to what with us is implied by a mode, and consists in determining the exact relative distances of the several sounds which constitute an octave, with respect to each other; while the *rágini* disposes of those sounds in a given succession, and determines the principal sounds. The same *tháta* may be adapted to several *ráginis*, by a different order of succession; whereas no *rágini* can be played but in its proper *tháta*."

Rága should not likewise be confounded with *gráma*; in a *gráma*, there may exist numerous *rágas*. It is rather similar to the English scale.

In the import attached to it by the sage *Bharata* and other *Sañskrita* authorities, *rága* signifies an effect on the mind, produced by the agreeable relation of successive notes; each *rága* having some affinity with certain feeling or affection of the mind. To all those that have no insight into Hindu music, this definition will not appear quite intelligible. We therefore attempt to define it in a manner which will enable them to understand the nature of the thing. By *rága* is implied the agreeable effect of any determinate succession of notes, employed with a strict regard to the laws of *bádi*, *sambádi*, *ánubádi* and *bibádi*, arranged with *múrchchhanás*, and of proportional lengths with respect to the nature of the *layá*, or the *ad libitum* movement that runs through its full time. It is not confined to regular measure. It has some resemblance to the melody of the ancient Greeks, which was conducted on the same principle as our *rágas*. In the composition of melody, as we have already stated, they were guided by the rules of melopœia which taught them to discern and choose those sounds which should be rejected, those which should be admitted, and those which should be most frequently employed. In our *rágas*, we also observe the same rule. With reference to its influence on the human mind, the melody was classified into three species; namely, the *systaltic*, the *diastaltic*, and the *enchastic*. Our *rágas* likewise vary according to different *rásas* or sentiments. These are usually enumerated *śriṅgára* or love, *hásya* or mirth, *karuná* or tenderness, *raudra* or anger, *víra* or heroism, *bhayánaka* or terror, *vibhatsa* or disgust, and *adbhuta* or surprise.

With regard to their composition, the *rágas* and their variations are divided into three *jati* or species: *śuddha*, *śálaṅka*, and *sañkírna*.

The *śuddha rágas* are such as are simple and original; the *sálaṅka* are those that bear an impress of some other *rága;* and the *saṅkírṇa* are such as are compounded of *śuddha* and *sálaṅka.* These are again sub-divided into three classes; namely, *sampúrṇa, oṛaba* and *kháṛaba.* All those *rágas* whose scale consists of seven notes, in any fixed succession whatever, come under the first class; those whose scale comprises six notes, belong to the second class; and those whose scale is composed of five notes, fall into the last class.

The three prominent notes in each *rága* are called *graha, nyása,* and *aṅśa.* The note with which a *rága* begins, is named *graha;* that in which it ends, *nyása;* and that which is most frequently used and predominates over all the other notes, *aṅśa.* The latter is the same as *bádi,* and is the origin of the *graha* and *nyása.* According to the *Saṅskṛita* authorities, the same note should be the *graha* and *nyása;* but in modern practice, this rule is not strictly observed.

Rágas are not sung more than once in their simple form, but are varied on their repetition by *tánas,* performed by means of *múrchchhanás* and *gamakas.* These are not considered essential to *rágas,* but are introduced to embellish them according to the pleasure of the performer, with this restriction that in such graces, he should always confine himself to peculiar notes of the *rágas.* It should be observed in passing that in the formation of a *rága,* at least five notes are required; while two notes may go to constitute a *tána.* *Tánas,* as applied to *rágas,* are of a similar nature to those of a song, with this chief distinction that in the former they do not follow any regular measure; whereas in the latter they do so. Of *tánas* there are two species: *śuddha* and *kuta*, each comprising a great variety of styles.

It is a practice with singers, before commencing a song, to develop the character of the *rága* to which it is set, by means of *gamakas, múrchchhanás* and *tánas*. Such a practice is called *alápa*, in which the performer should adhere to the notes peculiar to the *rága*, and pay strict attention to the laws of *bádi, samvádi, anubádi*, and *bibádi*, as also to *añśa, graha*, and *nyása*. In *alápa*, there is no fixed rule with regard to *tála*; but the notes should be of proportional lengths with respect to the nature of the *laya*, or the *ad libitum* movement that runs through its full time. *Alápa* like *gita* is arranged into four parts, called *barnas*. The first part where the notes glide on slowly so as to manifest the character of the *rága*, is called the *asthayi*; the second part where the singer ascends to a higher scale, the *antará*; the third where both *asthayi* and *antará* are blended together, the *sanchári*; and the fourth where the *rága* is dropped, *ábhoga*.

Rága, when rhythm is given to it, receives the character of *gita*, the essential elements of the latter being notes and *mátrás*. The name of *gita* applies to all measured strain of music, whether vocal or instrumental. The most essential characteristics of *kanta-gita* or vocal music are *ragánga, bhashánga* and *kriánga*; *i.e., rága*, language and activity of execution; while all other qualifications required in it, pass under the name of *upánga*, or secondary characteristics. These, when combined with good taste, compose the maximum of vocal excellence. Of vocal music, there are various styles, such as *svaragráma*, *tribata*, *visnupada*, *dhrubapada*, and many others.

There are four principal systems of *Sañskrita* music, of which the first is derived from *Brahmá*; the second from *Bharata*; the third from *Hanumanta*; and the four from *Kalvinatha*. The best and most primitive of these systems is that of *Brahmá*. Besides these, there are several other minor systems, such as those of *Matañgaja*, *Kahala*, *Somesvara*, *Devarája*, *Kshetrarája*, *Bhojarája*, *&c.* These are all very ancient, and have been deduced from the four principal ones. On the aforesaid systems, primary and secondary, again, have been built many excellent and valuable works on music, among which the *Sañgita Darpana* by *Damodaramiśra*, the *Sañgita Náráyana* by *Náráyanadeva*, the *Sañgita Ratnákara* by *Sárañgadeva*, and the *Narttaka Nirnaya* by *Pundarika Bichchhala* are much extant among us.

But we find a diversity of opinion as to the system, according to which music has all along been practised. In fact, we do not conform to any particular system in our present practice, but are guided by rules and directions from various authorities.

In the opinion of the best and greatest of authorities, the six original *rágas* are named *Śrírága*, *Vasanta*, *Panchama*, *Bhairava*, *Megha* and *Nattanáráyana*, and are restricted for their performance to particular times and seasons. They are each represented as a demi-god, wedded to six *rágińis* or nymphs. We shall give their personifications and descriptions in the course of the book.

Before we finish this Introduction, a few observations need to be made on the Indian system of notation, and a description of the signs and symbols that have been used in this book, should be given. The notation extant among us is not a recent invention, but is found to occur in the *Rágabibodha*—a fact which proves that it has its origin in an age beyond the light of authentic history. As a proof of its antiquity, we beg to refer you to a printed form of notation, written in the oldest *Sañskṛita* character, of *Vasantarága* in Sir William Jones' Musical Modes of the Hindus in the Asiatic Researches. Owing partly to long disuse, and partly to the loss of authorities, the notation has come down to us in a crippled form, many of its signs and symbols having become obsolete, or having been buried in the depth of time. Had it not been the case, the practice of *Sañskṛita* music would not have been almost wholly lost, and its rich treasures would not have suffered so much wreck. To impart our music in its present form, a permanent character, and to facilitate the acquisition of its knowledge, we have thought it advisable to revive our ancient national notation, with such modifications and improvements as are necessary for adapting it to modern requirements.

In imitation of the original *Sañskṛita* notation, we represent our modern music by means of one line, with the initials of the seven notes, and with certain signs suited for the purpose. We have also three-lined notation extant among us. This is an innovation introduced by Professor Kshetra Mohana Goswamí, for the reason that the three *saptakas* to which Hindu music is confined, are very aptly represented by three lines; the notation in one line is however sanctioned by ancient usage. We might be asked the reason why we do not introduce the English system of notation into our music. To this we reply that European music being of a different nature from Hindu music, the notation that obtains in the former is quite unfit for representing the latter. It is generally admitted that every civilized nation that has a music of its own, has also a peculiar system of notation for representing it. Whatever the nature and form of that system, be it a rude, or be it an advanced one, it is well adapted to the peculiarities of the music it is intended to express, and can by no means be aptly rendered into the notation of another nation, however improved and scientific it may be, without the latter being subjected to some modifications. Our system of notation, it must be observed, is simple and convenient, and satisfies all practical requirements. If we were to adopt the English notation with some modifications for *śrutis*, some more for *múrchchhanás* and various other graces, and some more for a great variety of *tálas*, *&c.*, how cumbrous and complicated it would appear! Surely, it would be more difficult of comprehension than our national system.

The notes constituting a *saptaka*, are generally indicated by *sa*, *ṛi*, *ga*, *ma*, *pa*, *dha*, *ni*, which respectively correspond with the notes of the *diatonic* scale, C, D, E, F, G, A, B.

The three *saptakas*, which are commonly used in Hindu music, are represented in the *stabaka* or staff below:—

C D E F G A B C D E F G A B C D E F G A B.

The first seven notes that have the dots *under* them, belong to the *mandra* or lower *saptaka*; the next seven notes to the *madhya* or middle *saptaka*; and the last seven notes that have the dots *over* them to the *tára saptaka*. Among the three *saptakas*, the *madhya saptaka* is the standard. If we require to note down *saptakas* higher or lower than the three already shown, as many dots must be used *over* or *under* the notes as they are higher or lower than the middle or standard *saptaka*. Thus, the note $\ddot{C}$ would indicate that this $\ddot{C}$ is two *saptakas* higher than the corresponding note of the *madhya saptaka*, or one *saptaka* higher than the corresponding one of the *tára saptaka*. Similarly, C would show that this C is two *saptakas* lower than the corresponding note of the middle *saptaka*, or one *saptaka* lower than the similar one of the *mandra saptaka*.

The three *saptakas* noted down in the above staff, are sufficient for the purpose of our vocal music. The provision for more *saptakas* than three is required for representing instrumental music, or the music of other nations.

The *patáká* (ᒥ) is the sign for *tívra swaras* or sharps, and the *trikona* (△) is for *komala swaras* or flats, both of which are placed upon the notes. Thus, $\overset{\text{ᒥ}}{F}$ stands for F sharp, and $\overset{\Delta}{D}$ for D flat

When the signs for *tívras* and *komalas* have a dot upon their head, they represent *atitívra* (very sharp) and *atikomala* (very flat). Thus $\overset{\dot{\text{ᒥ}}}{F}$

stands for very sharp F, and D for very flat D. *Atitivra* and *atikomala* are the minute divisions of notes used in some of our melodies.

There are, let us recapitulate, three species of *mátrás;* namely *rhaswa dirgha* and *pluta*. The measure of time in pronouncing a short vowel, is called the *rhaswa mátrá; dirgha mátrá* is twice the length of a short vowel, and *pluta mátrá*, three or more times the length of a short vowel. They are respectively represented by one, two and three or more perpendiculars, which are placed upon the notes; thus C, C, and C, D, &c., &c., *rhaswa mátrá* is again divided into *ardha* (*i. e.*, half) and *anu* (*i. e.*, quarter) *mátrás*. The sign (◡) for *ardha-mátrá*, called in *Sañskrita ardha-chandra-chinha* or crescent, and that (×) for *anu-mátrá*, called in *Sañskrita dhamaru-chinha*, are placed upon the note; thus, C D C D C D &c., &c.

If two or three notes are written in one place, but if the sign for *mátrá* falls only upon the first note, and the notes that succeed it are tied together by a sign of *bandhani* ( ), all the notes placed after the first note, should be expressed according to the value of that note; *e. g.*, C D E. Again, if one or two notes are tied together by the sign of *bandhani*, but are not marked with the sign of *mátrá*, the sign of *mátrá* falls upon a separate note placed after them. In such case, the note on which the sign of *mátrá* is given, embraces its previous notes in the same proportion of time, *e. g.*, CD E. Sometimes, the sign of *mátrá* falls in an empty place—a place where there is no note. In such case, time must be allowed up to the vacant place; *e.g.*, C D E F.

Tálas are formed from simple, compound and broken *mátrás*, from the various arrangements of which, they derive their different names; *e.g.*, nine *mátrás* constitute the *tála* named *ára*; six *ektála*, &c., &c.,

Tála consists of two principal actions; namely, *ágháta* and *birámа*—the beating and the rest. The sign of the former (ʾ) and that (∘) of the latter are placed upon the sign of *mátrá*; thus:—C, C.

According to *Sañskrita* music, the first beating of a *tála* is named *sama*, the sign of which (+) lies upon the sign of *mátrá*, and is represented thus:—C. The space of time from *sama* to *biráma* is called in *Sañskrita* a *mancha*. Every *mancha*, according to the number of *mátrá*, is divided by perpendicular lines, called *bibhájaka rekhá* (|), which might be expressed in English as bars.

The *padma chinha* (::) or the sign of the lotus-flower indicates the completion of a melody, a song or an air.

EXAMPLES OF *TÁLAS* USED IN THIS BOOK.

Drutatritáli or 4 mátrás to the bar.

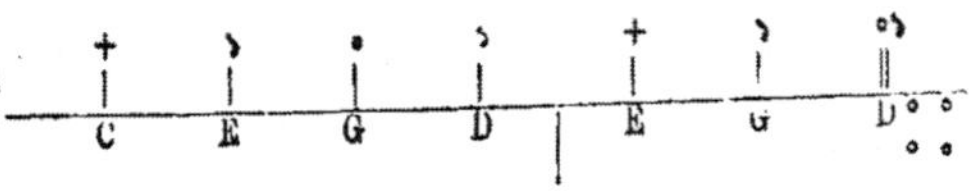

Madhyamána or 8 *mátrás* to the bar.

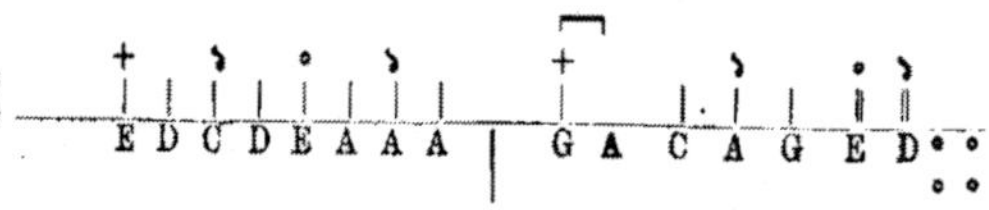

Sitalhatritáli or 16 *mátrás* to the bar.

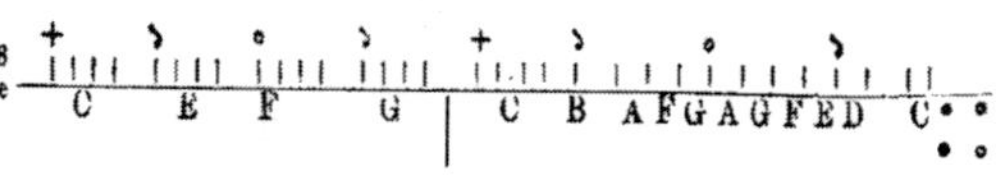

Ektálá or 6 *mátrás* to the bar.

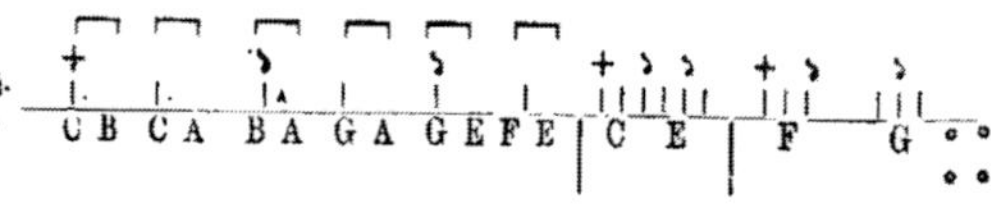

Ará or 9 *mátrás* to the bar.

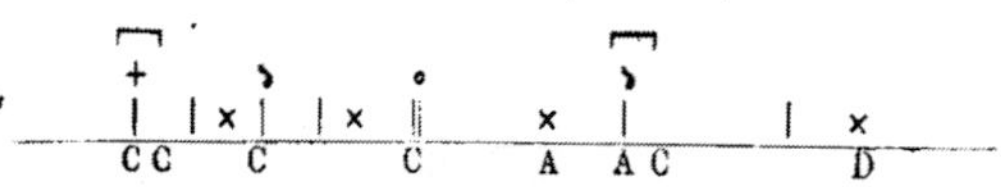

In vocal music, the words of a song are put exactly under the notes in which they are to be sung. But if it is found in the notation, that a note or a number of notes have no word or words to be expressed, the note of the previous word should be made to gradually glide through the note or notes that have not the corresponding words under them,—without stopping the voice, and according to the given time. In such case, the notes that have no words under them will have dots instead; thus,

C D E F. It will be sung

Ha . . .

exactly as if it were C D E F.

Ha a a a.

Six Principal Ragas of the Hindus.

Lith and print by Kristobury Dass

Calcutta March 1876

SRÍ RAGA.

श्रीरागस्यध्यानम्।

लीलाविहारेण वनान्तराले चिन्वन् प्रसूनानि वधूसहायः।

विलासवेशो धृतदिव्यमूर्त्तिः श्रीराग एषः कथितः कवीन्द्रैः॥

The Meditation of Sri Raga.

The demi-god Sri Rága famed all over the earth sweetly sports with his nymph, gathering fresh blossoms in the bosom of yon grove, and his divine lineaments are distinguished through his graceful vesture.

This Rága is sung in the Dewy Season, generally in the evening.

SRÍ RÁGA.

TÁLA ÁṚÁ.

(D F A)

ÁSTHÁYÍ

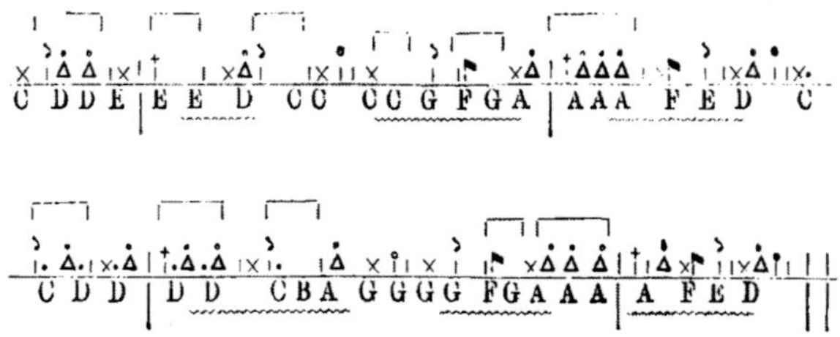

Antará.

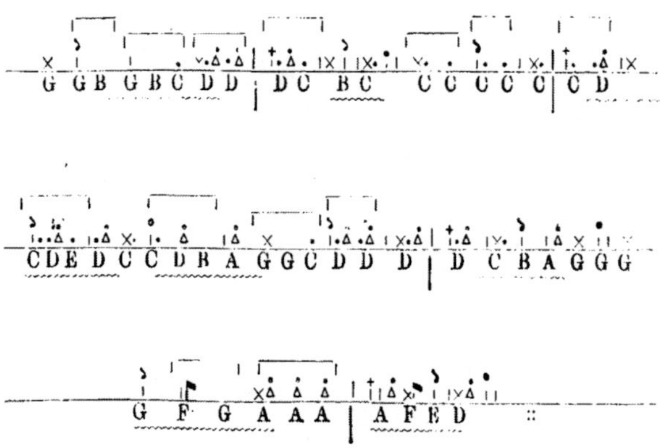

Six Principal Rágas of the Hindus.

(1)

Śrírága.

Of the six original *rágas*, *Śrírága* is the first. Its performance is restricted to the dewy season. It is a practice with us to sing it at the close of the day, with the use of three *vikṛitas:* a-very flat, d-very flat, and f-sharp. There is no necessity of f-natural in its performance. Quartertones enter into its composition, d and a being rendered three *śrutis* lower than in the *sharjagráma*. It belongs to the class, called *sampúrna*. It has c for its *bádí*, and d-very flat for its *sambádí*, while it begins and ends with c. Some of the musicians sing it with d-very flat as its *bádí* and a-very flat as its *sambádí*. In Southern India it is performed at noon with the omission of e and a.

Six Principal Ragas of the Hindus.

Lith and Print by Kristohury Doss   BASANTA   Calcutta.

वसन्तरागस्य ध्यानम् ।

चूताङ्कुरैश्चैव कृतावतंसो विघूर्णमानारुणपद्मनेत्रः ।

पीताम्बरः काञ्चनचारुदेहो वसन्तरागो युवतीप्रियश्च ॥

The Meditation of Basanta Rága.

This Rága is represented as being of a golden hue, dressed in yellow garments and having his ears ornamented with the blossoms of the mango. His lotus-like eyes are rolling round and are of the colour of the rising Sun. He is loved by the females.

This Rága is sung in the Spring.

BASANTA.

TÁLA ÁRÁ.

(D F)

ÁSTHÁYÍ

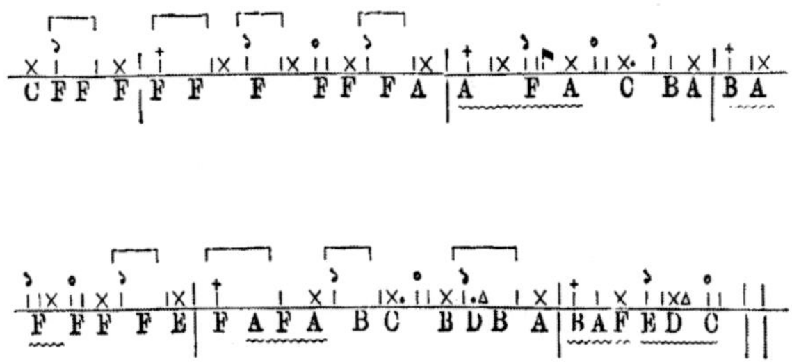

Antará.

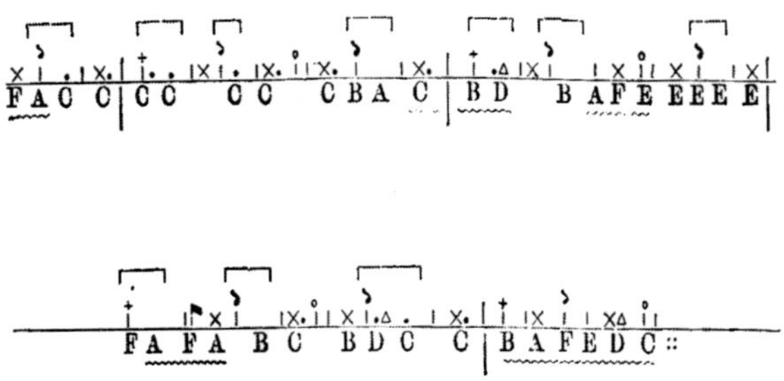

(2)

Vasanta.

Of the six principal *rágas*, *Vasanta* is the second. It is assigned for its performance to the spring. It is sung with the use of two *vikritas*: d-flat and f-sharp, and with the omission of g. It belongs to the class, called *shárraba*, and has f for its *bádí* and c for its *sambádí*. It begins and ends with c.

Six Principal Ragas of the Hindus.

Lith: and Print: by Kristobury Doss. BHAIRABA. Calcutta.

भैरवरागस्य ध्यानम्।

गङ्गाधरः शशिकलातिलकस्त्रिनेत्रः सर्पैर्विभूषिततनुर्गजकृत्तिवासाः।

भास्वत्त्रिशूलकर एष नृमुण्डधारी शुभ्राम्बरो जयति भैरवरागराजः।

The Meditation of Bhairaba Raga.

The representation of this Rága mostly resembles that of Mahádev. He bears the Gangá on his head. His forehead is adorned with the crescent moon. He has three eyes. His body is encircled all over with serpents. He wears white clothes. Holds a shining trident in one hand, and human skull in the other.

This Rága is sung in the Autumn.

Six Principal Rágas of the Hindus.

BHAİRABA.

TÁLA EKATÁLÁ.

(B D A)

ÁSTHÁYÍ

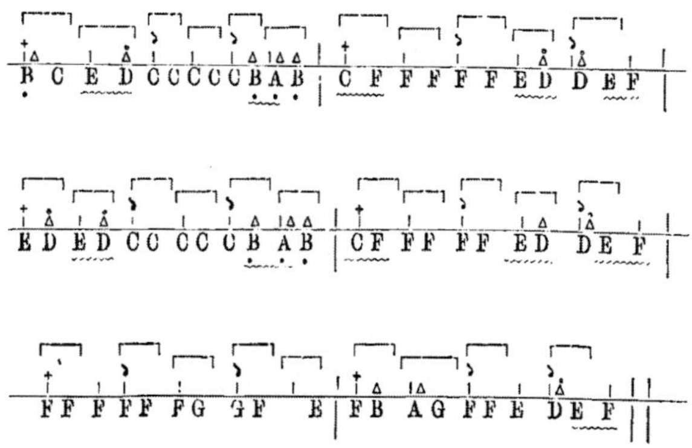

Antará.

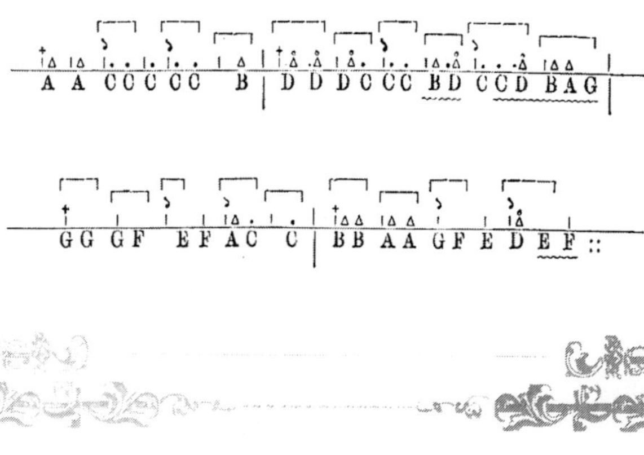

(3)

Bhairava.

Of the six original *rágas, Bhairava* is the third. By some its performance is assigned to autumn, and by others to summer. In our modern practice, however, this *rága* is not exclusively restricted to any particular season, but is sung in the morning of all the seasons. It is performed with the use of d-very flat, a-flat, b-flat. Herein also we find the application of quartertones. This *rága* belongs to the *sampúrṇa jati*, and has f for its *bádí* or *añsá*, and c for its *sambádí*. It begins with b and generally ends with c; but here it terminates with the *añsa*.

Six Principal Ragas of the Hindus.

Lith. and Print by Kristohury Doss. PANCHAMA. Calcutta

पञ्चमरागस्य ध्यानम्।

रक्ताम्बरो रक्तविशालनेत्रः शृङ्गारयुक्तस्तरुणो मनस्वी।

सदा विभात्येष हि पञ्चमोऽयं योषित्प्रियः कोकिलमञ्जुभाषी॥

The Meditation of Panchama Rága.

This Rága is described as having large red eyes wearing red clothes, young, intelligent and of an amorous disposition.

This Rága is sung in the Summer.

PAṈCHAMA.

TÁLA ÁRÁ.

(D)

ÁSTHÁYÍ

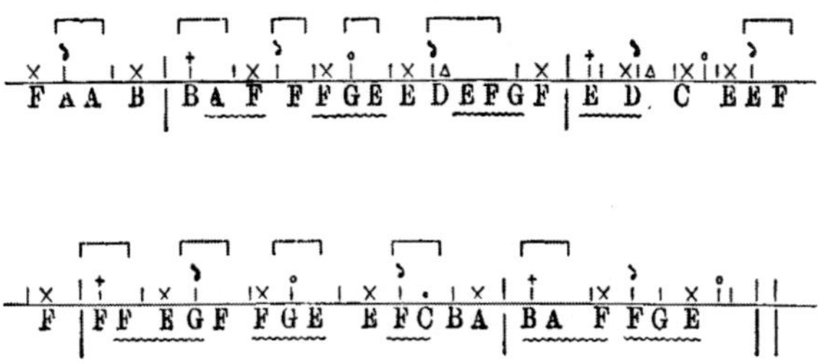

Antará.

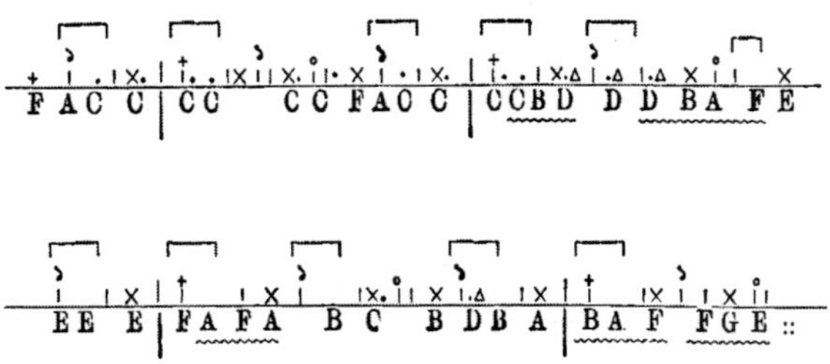

(4)

Panchama.

Of the six original *rágas*, *Panchama* is the fourth. In the opinion of some of the *Sañskrita* writers, its performance is considered opportune at autumn; in that of others, at summer. However, in practice, it is sung at the close of the night. There is a diversity of opinion as to the class it belongs to, some singing it in a scale comprising seven notes, others with the omission of g. In our performance, we conform to the former practice. In this *rága*, only one *vikrita*, namely d-flat, is used. It has f for its *bádi* or *añśa*, and c for its *sambádi*. It begins with the *añśa* and terminates with e.

Six Principal Ragas of the Hindus.

Lith: and Prints by Kristohury Doss MEGHA. Calcutta.

मेघरागस्य ध्यानम्।

विहारशीलोऽप्यतिनीलदेहो गभीरवादी प्रियकामिनीभिः।

कामातुरः पिङ्गलनेत्रयुग्मो मल्लाररागो गजवाहनोऽयम्॥

The Meditation of Megha Rága.

This Rága is represented as being dressed in blue garments. Has a grave voice and violet eyes. Rides on an elephant, and is sung in the rainy Season.

Six Principal Rágas of the Hindus.

MEGHA.

TÁLA EKATÁLÁ.

ÁSTHÁYÍ

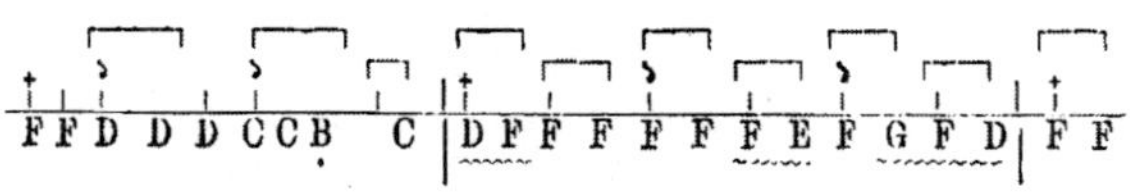

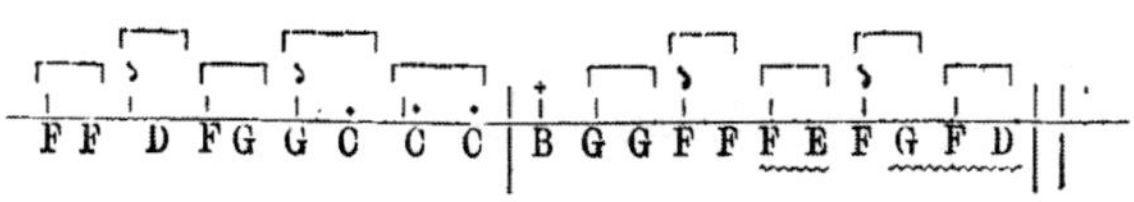

Antará.

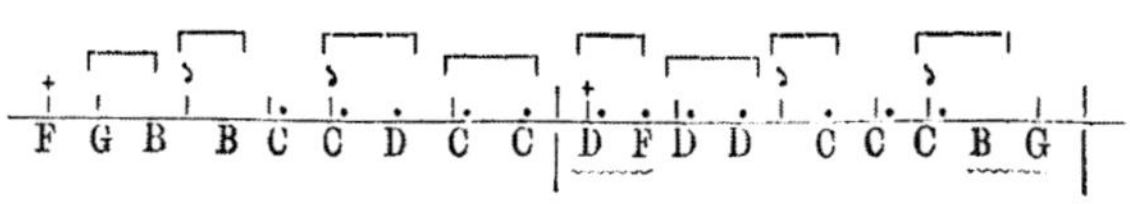

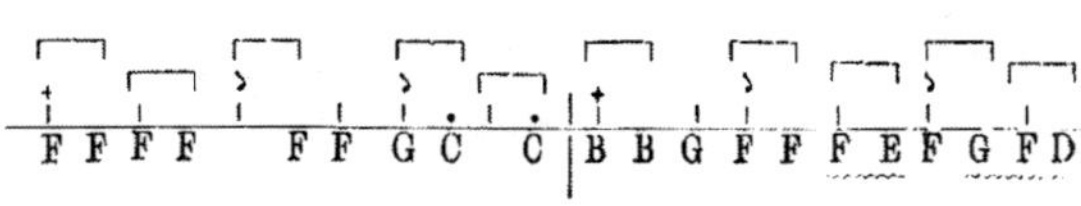

(5)

Megha.

Of the six principal *rágas*, *Megha* is the fifth. It is appropriated to the rainy season. This *rága* belongs to the class, called *shárabá*, it being generally sung with the omission of a. It has f for its *bádi* or *añśa*, and both c and d for its *sambádi* notes; while it begins with the *añśa*.

Six Principal Ragas of the Hindus.

Lith and Print by Kristohury Doss

NATTA NARAYAṆA.

Calcutta

नट्टनारायणरागस्य ध्यानम्।

तुरङ्गमस्कन्धनिबद्धबाहुः स्वर्णप्रभः शोणितशोणगात्रः।
संग्रामभूमौ विचरन् प्रतापी नटोऽयमुक्तः किल रक्तमूर्तिः॥

The Meditation of Nat-Náráyan Rága.

This Rága is personified as a mighty warrior, riding on horse back in the battle-field and clasping the neck of the animal with one of his arms. His body is all besmeared with blood.

This Rága is sung in the Winter.

NATTA NÁRÁYANA.

TÁLA ÁRÁ.

ÁSTHÁYI

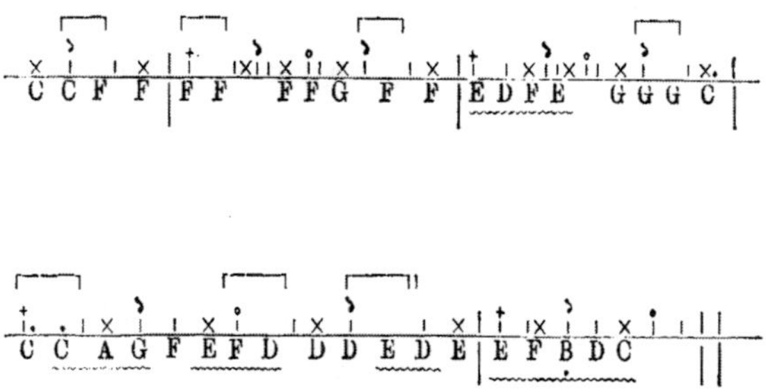

Antará.

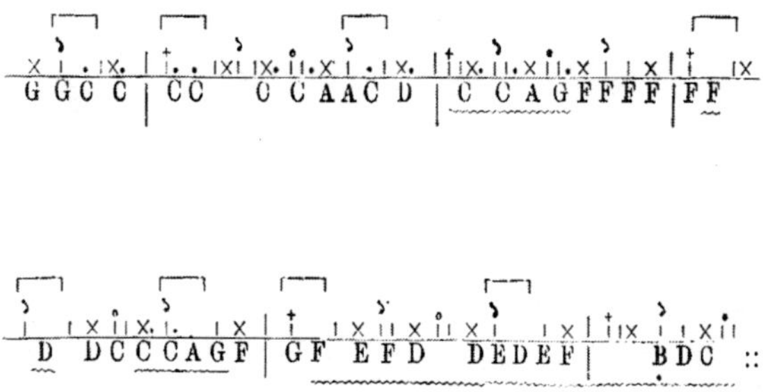

(6)

Nattanáráyana.

Nattanáráyana, otherwise called *Brihannat,* is the last. Its performance is restricted to winter. Songs set to it, are of rare use among us. It is a matter of no small difficulty for the performers to preserve it from being blended with the preceding *rága.* It has f for its *bádi* or leading note, and c for its *sambádi.* It begins and ends with c.

Six Principal Rágas of the Hindus.

These emblematical representations of the six *rágas* are expressive of the seasons at which their performance is considered opportune, and of the feelings they are intended to awaken in the mind. These *rágas* are all marked by a flowing ease on which their beauty hinges. Varied as they are by different sentiments, it would be doubtless interesting to characterize them. In *Śrí*, the prevailing passion is love; mildness and mirth are its principal characteristics. It may also be adapted to the expression of the heroic sentiment. *Vasanta* is also characterized by love. It is gay and sprightly. The predominant character of *Bhairava* is gravity. It is grand and contemplative, and is adapted to subjects of a sublime nature. In *Panchama*, love prevails. It is rich, feminine and delicate. *Megha* is suited to the expression of love as well as of heroism. It is solemn and grave. *Nattanáráyana* is characterized by the heroic as well as by sentiment of surprise. It is bold, vigorous and commanding.

It should, in conclusion, be remarked that our *rágas* and *ráginis* in general are marked by tender feelings. The fact might be accounted for by physical and other adventitious circumstances. Our Arian ancestors of the North dwelling during the Vedic age on the lap of smiling nature, and having little experience of the evils of life, their tender feelings sprang up in their mind with vigor; while the mild influence of their climate favored their growth. Everywhere they felt "the voluptuous calm and the dreamy atmosphere of the lotus-eaters' land. Their social organization at the same time gave them an ample scope for the free exercise of their gentler passions. All gloomy ideas were drowned in the enjoyment of present happiness; the tenor of their soul is mirrored forth in their music." Again the want of foreign influence effectually preserved it from being mixed up with an exotic element; while the absence of any deep-stirring revolution within precluded the growth of the stronger passions. It may justly be asserted, therefore, that the Hindus are not very successful in the development of the heroic and other rougher passions—"those hardy children of *Western* Songs;" but in love and other gentler feelings, they have showed a marked success. Hindu music abounds in feeling and imagination; but for bolder passions, we must look where a colder climate displays a stronger race.

APPENDIX.

SONGS OF JAYADEVA.

बसन्तबाहार। (ऋ, ग, ध, नि।) सम्पूर्ण।

ताल मध्यमान।

ललितलवङ्गलतापरिशीलनकोमलमलयसमीरे
मधुकरनिकरकरम्बितकोकिलकूजितकुञ्जकुटीरे ॥
विहरति हरिरिह सरसवसन्ते
नृत्यति युवतिजनेन समं सखि विरहिजनस्य दुरन्ते ॥
उन्मदमदनमनोरथपथिकवधूजनजनितविलापे
अलिकुलसंकुलकुसुमसमूहनिराकुलबकुलकलापे ॥
मृगमदसौरभरभसवशंवदनवदलमालतमाले
युवजनहृदयविदारणमनसिजनखरुचिकिंशुकजाले ॥

Rága—Basantabáhára. Tála—Madhyamána.

ने ० ० न स मं ० ० ० स खि
ne — — na sa man — — — sa khi
बि र ० ० ० हि ज न स्य दु
bi ra — — — hi ja na sya du
र ० ० ० ० ० ० न्ते ० ० ० ल लि
ra — — — — — — nte — — — la li
त ल ब ङ्ग ल ता ० ० प रि
ta la ba ṅga la tá — — pa ri
शी ० ० ल न ० ० ० को ० म ल म ल
śi — — la na — — — ko — ma la ma la
य स ० मी ० ० ० ० ० ० रे ०
ya sa — mí — — — — — — re —

० ० म धु क र नि क र क
— — ma dhu ka ra ni ka ra ka
र ० ० म्बि त को ० कि ल कू ० ० ०
ra — — mbi ta ko — ki la kú — — —
जि त कु ञ्ज कु ० टी ० ० ०
ji ta ku nja ku — tí — — —
० ० ० रे ० ० ० उ म्म द
— — — re — — — — mma da
म द न म नो ० र थ प थि
ma da na ma no — ra tha pa thi
क ब धू ० ज न ज नि त बि
ka ba dhú — ja na ja ni ta bi

lá — — — pe a li ku la sañ —
ku la ku su ma sa mú ha ui rá —
ku la ba ku la ka lá — pe mṛi ga
ma da sau ra bha ra bha sa ba śa —
mva da — na ba da la má — la ta —
má — — — — — — le — — — yu ba

मदनमहीपतिकनकदण्डरुचिकेशरकुसुमविकासे ।
मिलितशिलीमुखपाटलिपटलकृतस्मरतूणविलासे ॥ ४ ॥
विगलितलज्जितजगदवलोकनतरुणकरुणकृतहासे ।
विरहिनिकृन्तनकुन्तमुखाकृतिकेतकदन्तुरिताशे ॥ ५ ॥
माधविकापरिमलललिते नवमालिकयातिसुगन्धौ ।
मुनिमनसामपि मोहनकारिणि तरुणाकारणबन्धौ ॥ ६ ॥
स्फुरदतिमुक्तलतापरिरम्भणमुकुलितपुलकितचूते ।
वृन्दावनविपिने परिसरपरिगतयमुनाजलपूते ॥ ७ ॥
श्रीजयदेवभणितमिदमुदयति हरिचरणस्मृतिसारं ।
सरसवसन्तसमयवनवर्णनमनुगतमदनविकारं ॥ ८ ॥

सोहिनी (षू) खाड़व।

ताल मध्यमान।

निन्दति चन्दनमिन्दुकिरणमनुविन्दति खेदमधीरं।

व्यालनिलयमिलनेन गरलमिव कलयति मलयसमीरं॥

सा विरहे तव दीना।

माधव मनसिजविशिखभयादिव भावनया त्वयि लीना॥१॥

Sohiní. Túla—Madhyamána.

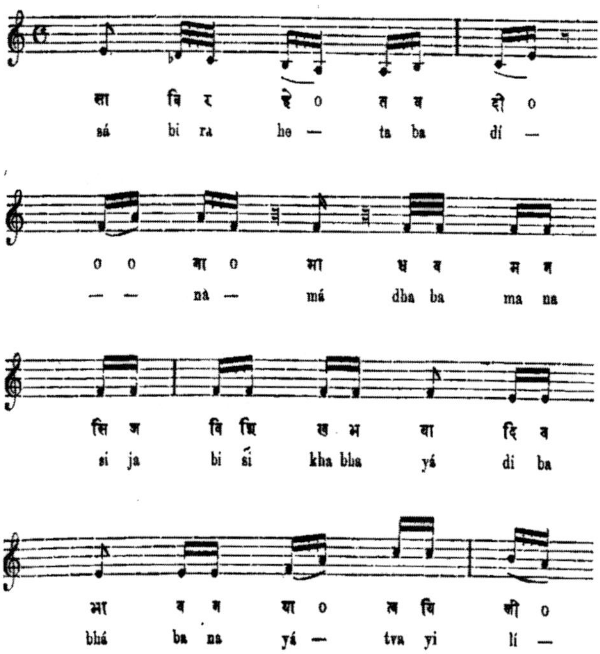

o o o o ना o ॥९॥
— — — — ná —
नि o o न्द ति च न्द न मि
ni — — nda ti cha nda na mi
न्दु कि र ण म नु बि न्द ति खे
ndu ki ra ṇa ma nu bi nda ti khe
द म धी o o रं o o o o ब्या
da ma dhí — — rañ — — — — byá
ल नि ल य मि ल ने o o न ग
la ni la ya mi la ne — — na ga
र ल मि ब क o ल य ति म ल य स
ra la mi ba ka — la ya ti ma la ya sa
मी o o o o o o रं o
mí — — — — — — rañ —

अविरलनिपतितमदनशरादिव भवदवनाय विशालं ।
स्वहृदयमर्म्मणि वर्म्म करोति सजलनलिनीदलजालं ॥ २ ॥
कुसुमविशिखशरतल्पमनल्पविलासकलाकमनीयं ।
व्रतमिव तव परिरम्भसुखाय करोति कुसुमशयनीयं ॥ ३ ॥
वहति च वलितविलोचनजलधरमाननकमलमुदारं ।
विधुमिव विकटविधुन्तुददन्तदलनगलितामृतधारं ॥ ४ ॥
विलिखति रहसि कुरङ्गमदेन भवन्तमसमशरभूतं ।
प्रणमति मकरमधो विनिधाय करे च शरं नवचूतं ॥ ५ ॥
प्रतिपदमिदमपि निगदति माधव तव चरणे पतिताहं ।
त्वयि विमुखे मयि सपदि सुधानिधिरपि तनुते तनुदाहं ॥ ६ ॥
ध्यानलयेन पुरःपरिकल्प्य भवन्तमतीव दुरापं ।
विलपति हसति विषीदति रोदिति चञ्चति मुञ्चति तापं ॥ ७ ॥
श्रीजयदेवभणितमिदमधिकं यदि मनसा नटनीयं ।
हरिविरहाकुलवल्लवयुवतिसखीवचनं पठनीयं ॥ ८ ॥

खाम्बावती (नि) सम्पूर्ण ।

ताल श्लथत्रिताली ।

सञ्चरदधरसुधामधुरध्वनिमुखरितमोहनवंशम् ।
वलितदृगञ्चलचञ्चलमौलिकपोलविलोलवतंसम् ॥
रासे हरिमिह विहितविलासम् ॥
स्मरति मनो मम कृतपरिहासम् ! ॥१ ।

Khámvábati. Tála Slathatritáli.

स 0 च र द ध र सु धा 0
Sa — ncha ra da dha ra Su dhá —
0 म धु र 0 ध्व नि मु ख रि त मो
— ma dhu ra — dhva ni mu kha ri ta mo
0 ह न बं 0 0 शं ब लि त
— ha na bañ — — śañ ba li ta
दृ ग च ल च 0 च ल मौ 0 लि
dri ga ṉcha la cha — ṉcha la mau — li
क पो ल बि लो 0 ल ब तं 0 0
ka po la bi lo — la ba tañ — —
0 0 0 0 0 0 सं 0 0 0 ॥१॥
— — — — — — sañ — — —

चन्द्रकचारुमयूरशिखण्डकमण्डलवलयितकेशम्।
प्रचुरपुरन्दरधनुरनुरञ्जितमेदुरमुदिरसुवेशम्॥२॥

गोपकदम्बनितम्बवतीमुखचुम्बनलम्भितलोभम्।
बन्धुजीवमधुराधरपल्लवमुल्लसितस्मितशोभम्॥३॥

विपुलपुलकभुजपल्लववलयितवल्लवयुवतिसहस्रम्।
करचरणोरसि मणिगणभूषणकिरणविभिन्नतमिस्रम्॥४॥

जलदपटलचलदिन्दुविनिन्दकचन्दनतिलकललाटम्।
पीनपयोधरपरिसरमर्दननिर्दयहृदयकवाटम्॥५॥

मणिमयमकरमनोहरकुण्डलमण्डितगण्डमुदारम्।
पीतवसनमनुगतमुनिमनुजसुरासुरवरपरिवारम्॥६॥

विशदकदम्बतले मिलितं कलिकलुषभयं शमयन्तम्।
मामपि किमपि तरङ्गदनङ्गदृशा मनसा रमयन्तम्॥७॥

श्रीजयदेवभणितमतिसुन्दरमोहनमधुरिपुरूपम्।
हरिचरणस्मरणं प्रति संप्रति पुण्यवतामनुरूपम्॥८॥

सारङ्ग (ग, ध विवादी) षाड़व ।

ताल श्लथ त्रिताली

पश्यति दिशि दिशि रहसि भवन्तम् ।
त्वदधरमधुरमधूनि पिबन्तम् ।
नाथ हरे सीदति राधा वासगृहे ॥ १ ॥
त्वदभिसरणरभसेन वलन्ती ।
पतति पदानि कियन्ति चलन्ती ॥ २ ॥
विहितविशदबिसकिसलयवलया ।
जीवति परमिह तव रतिकलया ॥ ३ ॥

Saranga. Túla Slathatritálí.

0 0 0 0 0 0 0 ना 0 0 0 0 थ ह
— — — — — — — ná — — — — tha ha
रे 0 प 0 श्य ति दि शि दि शि
re — pa — śya ti di śi di śi
र ह सि भ 0 0 ब 0 न्तं त्व द
ra ha si bha — — ba — ntañ tva da
ध र म धु 0 0 र म धू 0
dha ra ma dhu — — ra ma dhú —
नि पि ब 0 0 0 0 0 0 0
ni pi ba — — — — — — —
0 0 0 0 0 0 0 0 0 0 0 0 0
— — — — — — — — — — — — —

० ० ० ० ० ० न्तं ना ० ० ० ० थ ह
— — — — — — ntañ ná — — — — tha ha
रे ० सी त्व द भि स र ण ० ०
re — sí tva da bhi sa ra ṇa — —
र भ से ० न ब ल न्ती ० ०
ra bha se — na ba la nti — —
० प त ति प दा ० ० नि कि
— pa ta ti pa dá — — ni ki
य ० न्ति च ल ० ० ० ० न्ती ॥२॥
ya — nti cha la — — — — ntí
बि हि त बि श द बि श कि श
bi hi ta bi śa da bi śa ki śa

मुहुरवलोकितमण्डनलीला ।
मधुरिपुरहमिति भावनशीला ॥४॥
त्वरितमुपैति न कथमभिसारम् ।
हरिरिति वदति सखीमनुवारम् ॥५॥
श्लिष्यति चुम्बति जलधरकल्पम् ।
हरिरुपगत इति तिमिरमनल्पम् ॥६॥
भवति विलम्बिनि विगलितलज्जा ।
विलपति रोदिति वासकसज्जा ॥७॥
श्रीजयदेवकवेरिदमुदितम्
रसिकजनं तनुतामतिमुदितम् ॥८॥